The Best of May Maxim
Ripple Afghans

LEISURE ARTS, INC. • Maumelle, Arkansas

To The Point Throw

SHOPPING LIST

Yarn (Worsted Weight)

[6 ounces, 315 yards
(170 grams, 288 meters) per skein]:

- ☐ Color 1   Yellow - 1-2 skeins
- ☐ Color 2   Red - 1-2 skeins
- ☐ Color 3   Green - 1-2 skeins
- ☐ Color 4   Brown - 1-2 skeins
- ☐ Color 5   Blue - 1-2 skeins

Crochet Hook

- ☐ Size H-8 (5.00 mm)
  or size needed for gauge

SIZE INFORMATION

Size: 44" diameter (112 cm)

[62" diameter (157.5 cm)]

GAUGE INFORMATION

Rnds 1-10 = 9" (23 cm) diameter, measured from point to point, using suggested hook or any size hook which will give the correct stitch gauge.

── STITCH GUIDE ──

BEG CORNER - Work (ch 3, 2 dc, ch 3, 3 dc) in space indicated.

INSTRUCTIONS

Using Color 1, ch 8, join with sl st in first ch to form a ring.

Rnd 1: Ch 5 (counts as dc, ch 2), [dc in ring, ch 2] 7 times, join with sl st in 3rd ch of beg ch-5 - (8 ch-2 sps) Do not fasten off.

Rnd 2: Join Color 2 in any ch-2 sp, (sc, 3 dc, sc) in each ch-2 sp around, join with sl st in first sc - (8 small petals made) Fasten off.

Rnd 3: Using Color 1 and working behind petals, *ch 5, sl st between next 2 petals; rep from * around, join with sl st in first ch - (8 loops)

Rnd 4: (Sc, hdc, 3 dc, hdc, sc) in each loop around, join with sl st in first sc - (8 medium petals) Fasten off.

Rnd 5: Join Color 2 with sl st between any 2 petals of Rnd 4, *ch 5, sl st between next 2 petals; rep from * around, join with sl st in first sl st - (8 loops)

Rnd 6: (Sc, 4 dc, ch 1, 4 dc, sc) in each loop around, join with sl st in first sc - (8 large petals) Fasten off.

Rnd 7: Join Color 3 between any 2 petals, ch 7 (counts as tr, ch 3), tr in same sp, ch 2, sc in next ch-1 sp, ch 2, *(tr, ch 3, tr) in sl st between next 2 petals, ch 2, sc in next ch-1 sp, ch 2; rep from * around, join with sl st in 4th ch of beg ch-7.

Rnd 8: Sl st in next ch-sp, work Beg corner in same sp, *[3 dc in next ch-2 sp] twice**, *(3 dc, ch 3, 3 dc) in next ch-3 sp - corner made*; rep from * around, ending last rep at **, join with sl st in top of beg ch-3 - (8 corners) Fasten off.

Rnd 9: Join Color 4 in any ch-3 sp, (sc, ch 3, sc) in same sp, *ch 2, [sc between next 3-dc-group, ch 2] 3 times**, (sc, ch 3, sc) in next ch-3; rep from * around, ending last rep at **, join with sl st in first sc.

Rnd 10: Sl st in ch-3 sp, work Beg corner in same sp, *3 dc in next ch-2 sp, dc in next ch-2 sp, *yo, insert hook in same sp and draw up a loop, yo and draw through 2 loops on hook, yo, insert hook in next ch-2 sp and draw up a loop, yo and draw through 2 loops on hook, yo and draw through all 3 loops -* **Dec made over two ch-2 sps (counts as a 3-dc group),** dc in same sp as second half of Dec, 3 dc in next ch-2 sp**, corner in ch-3 sp of next corner; rep from * around, ending last rep at **, join with sl st in top of beg dc. Fasten off.

Rnd 11: Join Color 1 in any corner sp, (sc, ch 3, sc) in same sp, ch 2, *(sc, ch 2) between each 3-dc group across to next corner**, (sc, ch 3, sc) in next corner; rep from * around, ending last rep at **, join.

Rnd 12: Sl st in ch-3 sp, work Beg corner in same sp, *[3 dc in next ch-2 sp] twice, skip next ch-2 sp, [3 dc in next ch-2 sp] twice**, corner in next corner; rep from * around, ending last rep at **, join. Fasten off.

Rnd 13: Join Color 5 in any corner sp, (sc, ch 3, sc) in same sp, ch 2, *(sc, ch 2) between each 3-dc group across to next corner**, (sc, ch 3, sc) in next corner; rep from * around, ending last rep at **, join.

Rnd 14: Sl st in ch-3 sp, work Beg corner in same sp, *[3 dc in next ch-2 sp] twice, dc in next ch-2 sp, Dec over two ch-2 sps as before, dc in same sp as second half of Dec, [3 dc in next ch-2 sp] twice**, corner in next corner; rep from * around, ending last rep at **, join. Fasten off.

Rnd 15: Join Color 2 in any corner sp, (sc, ch 3, sc) in same sp, ch 2, *(sc, ch 2) between each 3-dc group across to next corner**, (sc, ch3, sc) in next corner; rep from * around, ending last rep at **, join.

Rnd 16: Sl st in ch-3 sp, work Beg corner in same sp, *[3 dc in next ch-2] 3 times, skip next ch-2 sp, [3 dc in next ch-2 sp] 3 times**, corner in next corner; rep from * around, ending last rep at **, join.

Rnd 17: Work as Rnd 13, using Color 3.

Rnd 18: Work as Rnd 14, but having one more 3-dc group on each side of each Dec.

Rnd 19: Work as Rnd 13, using Color 4.

Rnd 20: Work as Rnd 16, but having one more 3-dc group on each side of skip ch-2 sp.

Smaller Size Throw: Now continue in pattern as set in these last 4 rnds and rep color sequence as 1, 5, 2, 3 and 4, three times more. Fasten off. Weave in all ends

Larger Size Throw: Now continue in pattern as set in these last 4 rnds and rep color sequence as 1, 5, 2, 3 and 4, five times more, then Colors 1 and 5 once. Fasten off. Weave in all ends.

Optic Waves Throw

SHOPPING LIST

Yarn (Worsted Weight) 🧶 **MEDIUM 4**

[6 ounces, 315 yards
(170 grams, 288 meters) per skein]:

☐ Color 1   Green - 4 skeins

☐ Color 2   Natural - 4 skeins

Crochet Hook

☐ Size H-8 (5.00 mm)
  or size needed for gauge

SIZE INFORMATION

Size: 46 x 58" (117 x 147.5 cm)

GAUGE INFORMATION

One repeat = 7" [17.5 cm] wide and
10 rows = 5.5" [14 cm] at the point,
using suggested hook or any size
hook which will give the correct stitch
gauge.

── STITCH GUIDE ──

dc5tog: [yo, insert hook in next
st, yo and draw up a loop, yarn
over and draw through 2 loops
on hook] 5 times, yo and draw
through all 6 loops on hook.

INSTRUCTIONS

Using Color 1, ch 160.

Row 1: (right side) Work 2 dc in
4th ch from hook (beg 3 ch count
as first dc), ch 2, skip next 2 ch,
dc in each of next 8 ch, dc5tog,
dc in each of next 8 ch, ch 2,
*skip next 2 ch, 5 dc in next ch,
ch 2, skip next 2 ch,
dc in each of next 8 ch, dc5tog,
dc in each of next 8 ch, ch 2; rep
from * to last 3 ch, skip next 2 ch,
3 dc in last ch, turn - 133 dc.

Row 2: Ch 1, sc in each of first 3 dc,
2 sc in next ch-2 sp,
*sc in each dc across to next ch-2
sp, 2 sc in next ch-2 sp; rep from *
across to last 3 dc, sc in each of last
3 dc, turn - 157 sc.

Row 3: Ch 3 (counts as first dc
throughout), 2 dc in same st,
dc in each of next 2 sts, ch 2,
skip next 2 sts,
dc in each of next 6 sts, dc5tog,
dc in each of next 6 sts, ch 2,
*skip next 2 sts, dc in each of next
2 sts, 5 dc in next st,
dc in each of next 2 sts, ch 2,
skip next 2 sts, dc in each of next 6
sts, dc5tog,
dc in each of next 6 sts, ch 2; rep
from * to last 5 sts,
skip next 2 sts, dc in each of next 2
sts, 3 dc in last st, turn - 133 dc.

Row 4: Ch 1, sc in each of first 5
sts, 2 sc in next ch-2 sp,
*sc in each dc to next ch-2 sp,
2 sc in next ch-2 sp; rep from * to
last 5 sts, sc in each of last 5 sts,
turn - 157 sc.

Row 5: Ch 3, 2 dc in same st,
dc in each of next 4 sts, ch 2,
skip next 2 sts,
dc in each of next 4 sts, dc5tog,
dc in each of next 4 sts, ch 2,
*skip next 2 sts, dc in each of next
4 sts, 5 dc in next st, dc in each of
next 4 sts, ch 2, skip next 2 sts,
dc in each of next 4 sts, dc5tog,
dc in each of next 4 sts, ch 2; rep
from * to last 7 sts,

skip next 2 sts, dc in each of next 4 sts, 3 dc in last st, turn - 133 dc.

Row 6: Ch 1, sc in each dc and work 2 sc in each ch-2 sp across, turn - 157 sc.

Row 7: Ch 3, 2 dc in same st, dc in each of next 6 sts, ch 2, skip next 2 sts, dc in each of next 2 sts, dc5tog, dc in each of next 2 sts, ch 2, *skip next 2 sts, dc in each of next 6 sts, 5 dc in next st, dc in each of next 6 sts, ch 2, skip next 2 sts, dc in each of next 2 sts, dc5tog, dc in each of next 2 sts, ch 2; rep from * to last 9 sts, skip next 2 sts, dc in each of next 6 sts, 3 dc in last st, turn - 133 dc.

Row 8: As Row 6.

Row 9: Ch 3, 2 dc in same st, dc in each of next 8 sts, ch 2, skip next 2 sts, dc5tog, ch 2, *skip next 2 sts, dc in each of next 8 sts, 5 dc in next st, dc in each of next 8 sts, ch 2, skip next 2 sts, dc5tog, ch 2;

rep from * to last 11 sts, skip next 2 sts, dc in each of next 8 sts, 3 dc in last st, turn - 133 dc.

Row 10: As Row 6, changing to Color 2 in last st, turn. Break Color 1 and fasten off.
**Using Color 2, continue as follows:

Row 11: Ch 3, 2 dc in same st, ch 2, skip next 2 sts, dc in each of next 8 sts, dc5tog, dc in each of next 8 sts, ch 2, *skip next 2 sts, 5 dc in next st, ch 2, skip next 2 sts, dc in each of next 8 sts, dc5tog, dc in each of next 8 sts, ch 2; rep from * to last 3 sts, skip next 2 sts, 3 dc in last st, changing to Color 1 in last st, turn - 133 dc.

Row 12: Using Color 1, work as Row 2, changing to Color 2 in last st, turn - 157 sc.

Row 13: Using Color 2, work as Row 3, changing to Color 1 in last st, turn.

Row 14: Using Color 1, work as Row 4, changing to Color 2 in last st, turn.

Row 15: Using Color 2, work as Row 5, changing to Color 1 in last st, turn.

Row 16: Using Color 1, work as Row 6, changing to Color 2 in last st, turn.

Row 17: Using Color 2, work as Row 7, changing to Color 1 in last st, turn.

Row 18: Using Color 1, work as Row 6, changing to Color 2 in last st, turn.

Row 19: Using Color 2, work as Row 9, changing to Color 1 in last st, turn.

Row 20: Using Color 1, work as Row 6, changing to Color 2 in last st, turn.

Rows 21-30: Using Color 2 only, rep Row 11, then Rows 2-10, changing to Color 1 in last st of Row 10, turn.

Row 31: Using Color 1, work as Row 11, changing to Color 2 in last st, turn.

Row 32: Using Color 2, work as Row 2, changing to Color 1 in last st, turn - 157 sc.

Row 33: Using Color 1, work as Row 3, changing to Color 2 in last st, turn.

Row 34: Using Color 2, work as Row 4, changing to Color 1 in last st, turn.

Row 35: Using Color 1, work as Row 5, changing to Color 2 in last st, turn.

Row 36: Using Color 2, work as Row 6, changing to Color 1 in last st, turn.

Row 37: Using Color 1, work as Row 7, changing to Color 2 in last st, turn.

Row 38: Using Color 2, work as Row 6, changing to Color 1 in last st, turn.

Row 39: Using Color 1, work as Row 9, changing to Color 2 in last st, turn.

Row 40: Using Color 2, work as Row 6, changing to Color 1 in last st, turn.

Rows 41-50: Using Color 1 only, rep Row 11, then Rows 2-10, changing to Color 2 in last st of Row 10, turn.**

Now rep from ** to ×× once more,

but do not change colors at end of last row worked.

Weave in all ends neatly and securely.

Border: With right side of Throw facing, join Color 2 with sl st in upper left corner,

*work 3 sc in corner,

working across side edge, work 2 sc around ends of each dc or ch-3 and one sc in end of each sc row to next corner, work 3 sc in corner,

work 155 sc along short edge to next corner; rep from * once more, join with sl st in first sc. Fasten off.

Rnd 2: Join Color 1 with sl st in back loop of center sc of same corner, ch 3 (counts as first dc), dc in same st, now working in back loops only,

dc in each sc across to center sc of next corner, work 3 dc in corner sc, dc in each of next 14 sc (or until you are over the center of a dc5tog),

[work 5 dc in next sc, dc in each of next 10 sc, dc5tog (worked beneath the beg point of a triangle), dc in each of next 10 sc]

5 times,

work 5 dc in next sc, dc in each rem sc to center sc of next corner, work 3 dc in corner sc; rep from * to * once more,

[dc in each of next 10 sc (or until you are over a beg point of a triangle), dc5tog, dc in each of next 10 sts, 5 dc in next st] 5 times,

dc in each of next 10 sts, dc5tog, dc in each rem sc to beg corner, dc in beg corner, join with sl st in beg dc. Fasten off.

Rnd 3: Join Color 2 with sl st in back loop of center sc of any corner, ch 1, work 3 sc in same st, now working in back loops only, sc in each st around,

and 3 sc in center st of each corner, join with sl st in first sc. Fasten off.

Rnd 4: Join Color 1 with sl st in back loop of center sc of upper left corner, ch 3 (counts as first dc), dc in same st, now working in back loops only,

dc in each sc across to center sc of next corner, work 3 dc in corner sc, dc in each of next 19 sc (or until you are over center of previous shell of 5 dc),

[work 5 dc in next sc, dc in each of next 10 sc, dc5tog (worked over previous dc5tog), dc in each of next 10 sc] 5 times, work 5 dc in next sc, dc in each rem sc to center sc of next corner, work 3 dc in corner sc; rep from * to * once more,

[dc in each of next 10 sc, dc5tog (worked over previous dc5tog), dc in each of next 10 sts, 5 dc in next st] 5 times,

dc in each of next 10 sts, dc5tog, dc in each rem sc to beg corner, dc in beg corner,

join with sl st in beg dc. Fasten off.

Rnd 5: Joining Color 2 in upper left corner, work as Rnd 3. Do Not fasten off at end of rnd.

Rnd 6: Ch 2 (counts as hdc), working in back loops only, hdc in same st and in each st across to center sc of next corner, work 3 hdc in corner sc,

hdc in each sc until you are over the center of previous 5 dc Shell, 5 hdc in next sc,

[hdc in each of next 10 sc, dc5tog, hdc in each of next 10 sc, 5 hdc in next sc] 5 times, hdc in each rem sc before center sc of next corner, 3 hdc in corner sc,

hdc in each sc across to center sc of next corner, 3 hdc in corner sc,

hdc in each of next 10 sc (or until you can work over the previous dc5tog for the first one), dc5tog,

[hdc in each of next 10 sc, 5 hdc in next sc, hdc in each of next 10 sc, dc5tog] 5 times,

hdc in each rem sc to beg corner,

hdc in beg corner,

join with sl st in first hdc.

Fasten off.

Weave in all ends neatly and securely.

Autumn Waves Throw

■■■□ INTERMEDIATE

SHOPPING LIST

Yarn (Worsted Weight)

[6 ounces, 315 yards
(170 grams, 288 meters) per skein]:

- ☐ Color 1   Black - 2 balls
- ☐ Color 2   Camel - 2 balls
- ☐ Color 3   Brown - 2 balls
- ☐ Color 4   Burgundy - 2 balls

Crochet Hook

- ☐ Size J-10 (6.00 mm)
  or size needed for gauge

SIZE INFORMATION

Size: 37.5 x 51" (95 x 129.5 cm)

GAUGE INFORMATION

One repeat of 17 sts to 5.5" [14 cm] and 6 rows to 3.25" [8 cm] measured over pattern using suggested hook or any size hook which will give the correct stitch gauge.

── STITCH GUIDE ──

Puff st - [Yo, insert hook and draw up a loop] twice in same st, yo and draw through all 5 loops on hook.

dc2tog - [Yo, insert hook in next st, yo and draw up a loop, yo and draw through 2 loops on hook] twice, yo and draw through all loops on hook.

INSTRUCTIONS

Using Color 1, ch 121.

Foundation Row: (right side) Dc in 4th ch from hook, [dc2tog over next 2 ch] twice,
*[ch 1, Puff st in next ch] 5 times, ch 1,
[dc2tog over next 2 ch] 6 times; rep from * across to last 6 ch, ending last rep with [dc2tog over next 2 ch] 3 times, turn.

Row 1: Ch 1, sc in first st and in each st and ch-1 (not in space but into the ch-1) across to beg ch-3, turn, leaving beg ch-3 unworked. Break Color 1.

Row 2: Join Color 2 with sc in last sc of Row 1, ch 3, skip next st, dc in next st, [dc2tog] twice,
*[ch 1, Puff st in next st] 5 times, ch 1, [dc2tog] 6 times; rep from * across but ending last rep with [dc2tog] 3 times. Break Color 2.

Row 3: Turn, join Color 1 with sl st in last st of Row 2, work as Row 1 across. Break Color 1.

Repeat these last 2 rows twice more.

Now repeat Rows 2 and 3 three times more, but using Color 3 in place of Color 2 on every Row 2 worked.

Now repeat Rows 2 and 3 three times more, but using Color 4 in place of Color 2 on every Row 2 worked.

This completes one set of color - each section has 3 stripes of color (Row 2).

Now repeat these 18 rows 4 times more, ending after a Row 3 and do Not break yarn.

Next Row: Using Color 1, work as Row 2. Break yarn and fasten off.

Side Border: With right side facing, using Color 1, join to any corner of throw.

Work 140 sc evenly along side edge.

Finish off.

Repeat on other side of throw.

Rippled Lace Throw

■■■□ INTERMEDIATE

SIZE INFORMATION

Size: 47 x 58.5" (119.5 x 148.5 cm)

GAUGE INFORMATION

One repeat (from point to point) measures 4.25" [10.5 cm] wide and 6 rows to 4.5" [11.5 cm] measured over pattern, using suggested hook.

─── STITCH GUIDE ───

2-Dc Cluster: [Yo, insert hook in next st, yo & draw up a loop, yo & draw through 2 loops on hook] twice, yo, draw through all 3 loops on hook.

INSTRUCTIONS

Using Color 1, ch 213.

Row 1: Dc in 5th ch from hook, *[ch 1, skip next ch, dc in next ch] 3 times, ch 1, skip next ch, (dc, ch 3, dc) in next ch, [ch 1, skip next ch, dc in next ch] 3 times, ch 1, skip next ch**,

work 2-Dc Cluster working first dc in next ch, skip next 2 ch, work 2nd dc in next ch, yo and complete Cluster as given at left; rep from * across, ending last rep at **, work 2-Dc Cluster over last 3 ch (skip only one ch between dc), turn.

Row 2: Ch 3 (counts as dc), skip next ch-1 sp, dc in next dc, *[dc in next ch-1 sp, dc in next dc] 3 times, (2 dc, ch 3, 2 dc) in next ch-3, [dc in next dc, dc in next ch-1 sp] 3 times**,

work 2-Dc Cluster working first dc in next dc, skip next (ch 1, Cluster, ch 1), work 2nd dc in next dc, yo and complete Cluster; rep from * across, ending last rep at **, work 2-Dc Cluster over last 4 sts (skip ch-1 sp and dc between dc), working last dc in top of turning ch, yo and complete Cluster, turn.

Row 3: Ch 3 (counts as dc), skip first 2 sts, dc in next dc, *[ch 1, skip next dc, dc in next dc] 3 times, ch 1, (dc, ch 3, dc) in next ch-3, ch 1, [dc in next dc, ch 1, skip next dc] 3 times**,

work 2-Dc Cluster working first dc in next dc, skip next 3 sts, work 2nd dc in next dc, yo and complete Cluster; rep from * across, ending last rep at **, work 2-Dc Cluster over last 4 sts (skip only 2 sts between dc), working last dc in top of turning ch, yo and complete Cluster, turn.

Work Row 2 once more.

Now rep Rows 2 and 3 (beg with Row 3), for pattern AND AT THE SAME TIME, change colors as follows:

**Change to Color 2 & work 1 row.

Change to Color 1 & work 1 row.

Change to Color 2 & work 4 rows.

Change to Color 3 & work 1 row.

Change to Color 2 & work 1 row.

Change to Color 3 & work 4 rows.

Change to Color 1 & work 1 row.

Change to Color 3 & work 1 row.

Change to Color 1 & work 4 rows.**

Repeat from ** to ** 3 times more, but ending the last rep of Color 1 with 5 rows instead of 4.

Fasten off.

Bands of Lace Ripple

■■□□ EASY

SHOPPING LIST

Yarn (Worsted Weight) [4]

[6 ounces, 315 yards
(170 grams, 288 meters) per skein]:
☐ Wild Raspberry- 7 skeins

Crochet Hook

☐ Size I-9 (5.50 mm)
   or size needed for gauge

SIZE INFORMATION

Size: 46 x 62" (117 x 157.5 cm)

GAUGE INFORMATION

One repeat to 3.5" [9 cm] wide
and Rows 2-5 = 2.5" [6 cm] using
suggested hook or any size hook
which will give the correct stitch
gauge.

INSTRUCTIONS

Ch 222.

Row 1: Dc in 4th ch from hook,
ch 1, skip next ch, [dc in next ch,
ch 1, skip next ch] twice,
[dc, ch 1] 4 times in next ch,
[skip next ch, dc in next ch, ch 1]
twice,

*yo, skip next ch, insert hook in next
ch and draw up a loop, yo and draw
through 2 loops on hook,
yo, skip next 4 ch, insert hook in
next ch and draw up a loop, yo and
draw through 2 loops on hook,
yo and draw through all 3 loops on
hook - **counts as dc2tog**,
ch 1, skip next ch,
[dc in next ch, ch 1, skip next ch]
twice, [dc, ch 1] 4 times in next ch,
[skip next ch, dc in next ch, ch 1]
twice; rep from * to last 4 ch,
[yo, skip next ch, insert hook in
next ch and draw up a loop, yo
and draw through 2 loops on
hook] twice, yo and draw through
all 3 loops on hook, turn.

Row 2: Ch 3 (counts as first dc
throughout), skip next ch-1 sp,
[dc in next ch-1 sp, ch 1] 3 times,
[dc, ch 1] 4 times in next ch-1 sp,
dc in next ch-1 sp, [ch 1, dc in next
ch-1 sp] twice,
*skip next 2 ch-1 sps, [dc in next
ch-1 sp, ch 1] 3 times, [dc, ch 1] 4

times in next ch-1 sp,
dc in next ch-1 sp, [ch 1, dc in next
ch-1 sp] twice; rep from * across to
last ch-1 sp, skip last ch-1 sp, dc in
last dc, turn.

Row 3: Ch 3, skip next ch-1 sp,
[dc in next ch-1 sp, ch 1] 3 times,
[dc, ch 1] 4 times in next ch-1 sp,
dc in next ch-1 sp, [ch 1, dc in next
ch-1 sp] twice,
*skip next 2 ch-1 sps, [dc in next
ch-1 sp, ch 1] 3 times, [dc, ch 1] 4
times in next ch-1 sp,
dc in next ch-1 sp, [ch 1, dc in next
ch-1 sp] twice; rep from * across to
last ch-1 sp, skip last ch-1 sp, dc in
last dc, turn.

Row 4: Ch 3, skip next ch-1 sp, dc
in next dc, [dc in next ch-1 sp and
in next dc] 7 times,
*yo, insert hook in next ch-1 sp
and draw up a loop, yo and draw
through 2 loops on hook,
yo, insert hook in next ch-1 sp
and draw up a loop, yo and draw
through 2 loops on hook,

yo and draw through all 3 loops on hook - **dec made**, dc in next dc, [dc in next ch-1 sp and in next dc] 7 times; rep from * across to last ch-1 sp, skip last ch-1 sp and next dc, dc in last dc, turn.

Row 5: Ch 3, skip first 2 dc, [dc in next dc, ch 1, skip next dc] 3 times, [dc, ch 1] 4 times in next dc, skip next dc, dc in next dc, [ch 1, skip next dc, dc in next dc] twice, *skip next 3 sts, [dc in next dc, ch 1, skip next dc] 3 times, [dc, ch 1] 4 times in next dc, skip next dc, dc in next dc, [ch 1, skip next dc, dc in next dc] twice; rep from * to last 2 dc, skip next dc, dc in last dc, turn.

Now rep Rows 2-5 for pattern 20 times more (piece should measure about 57.5" [146 cm] from beg at this point), then rep Rows 2-4 once more.

Do not turn or fasten off after last row.

Border: Working around entire outside edge of Throw, ch 3, 2 dc in same st, work in dc evenly around, with 3 dc in each corner, join with sl st in top of beg ch-3. Be sure to work the same number of dc along each side of Throw, taking care that the edges do not pucker from too few sts or ripple from too many sts.

Break yarn and fasten off.

Weave in all ends securely.

Ocean Breeze Afghan

SHOPPING LIST

Yarn (Worsted Weight)

[3.5 ounces, 180 yards
(100 grams, 165 meters) per ball]:

☐ Main   Dk Blue - 7 balls
☐ Color 1 Lt Blue - 3 balls
☐ Color 2 Camel - 2 balls
☐ Color 3 Natural - 3 balls

Crochet Hook

☐ Size H-8 (5.00 mm)
    or size needed for gauge

SIZE INFORMATION

Size: 48 x 60" (122 x 152.5 cm)

GAUGE INFORMATION

One repeat measures 4" [10 cm] and 10 rows measures 4.5" [11.5 cm] using suggested hook or any size hook which will give the correct stitch gauge.

— STITCH GUIDE —

scCL - Draw up a loop in next stitch, skip next stitch, draw up a loop in next stitch, yo and draw through all 3 loops on hook.

dcCL - Yo, insert hook in next stitch and draw up a loop, yo and draw through 2 loops, skip next stitch, yo, insert hook in next stitch and draw up a loop, yo and draw through 2 loops, yo and draw through rem 3 loops on hook.

BegPuff - Beginning Puff Stitch: Insert hook in stitch indicated, draw loop up to .5", [yo, draw up .5" loop in same stitch] twice, yo and draw through 4 loops on hook, yo and draw through rem 2 loops.

Puff - Puff Stitch: Yo, draw up .5" loop in stitch indicated, yo, draw up .5" loop in same st, yo, draw through 4 loops on hook, yo and draw through rem 2 loops.

INSTRUCTIONS

Using MC, ch 170.

Row 1: (right side) Sc in 2nd ch from hook, sc in each of next 6 ch, 3 sc in next ch, *sc in each of next 13 ch, 3 sc in next ch; rep from * to last 7 ch, sc in each of last 7 ch, turn.

Row 2: Ch 3 (counts as first dc), skip next st, dc in each of next 6 sts, 3 dc in next st, *dc in each of next 6 sts, dcCL, dc in each of next 6 sts, 3 dc in next st; rep from * to last 8 sts, dc in each of next 6 sts, skip next st, dc in last st, turn.

Row 3: Ch 1, sc in first st, skip next st, sc in each of next 6 sts, *3 sc in next st, sc in each of next 6 sts, scCL, sc in each of next 6 sts; rep from * to last 9 sts, 3 sc in next st, sc in each of next 6 sts, skip next st, sc in top of beg ch, turn.

Row 4: Ch 1, BegPuff in first st, [ch 1, skip next 2 sts, Puff in next st] twice, *ch 2, skip next st, [Puff, ch 2] twice in next st, skip next st, [Puff in next st, ch 1, skip next 2 sts] 4 times, Puff in next st; rep from * to last 10 sts, ch 2, skip next st, [Puff, ch 2] twice in next st, skip next st, [Puff in next st, ch 1, skip next 2 sts] twice, Puff in last st, turn.

Row 5: Ch 1, sc in first Puff, [sc in next ch-sp, sc in next Puff] 3 times, *3 sc in next ch-sp, [sc in next Puff, sc in next ch-sp] 6 times, sc in next Puff; rep from * to last 4 ch-sps, 3 sc in next ch-sp, [sc in next Puff, sc in next ch-sp] 3 times, sc in last Puff changing to CC 1, turn.

Using CC 1, rep Rows 2 and 3, changing to CC 2 at the end of Row 3.

Using CC 2, [rep Row 3] twice, changing to CC 3 at end of second row.

Using CC 3, rep Rows 4 and 5, changing to MC at end of Row 5.

Using MC, rep Rows 2-5, changing to CC 1 at end of Row 5.

These last 10 rows set pattern and color sequence. Repeat these 10 rows 12 times more.

Break yarn and fasten off.

Weave in all ends.

Rise and Fall Throw

●●●◻ INTERMEDIATE

SHOPPING LIST

Yarn (Worsted Weight)

[6 ounces, 315 yards
(170 grams, 288 meters) per skein]:

☐ Color A Pagoda - 3 skeins
☐ Color B Aqua Mist - 1 skein
☐ Color C Chocolate - 1 skein
☐ Color D Autumn Mist - 1 skein
☐ Color E Celestial - 1 skein
☐ Color F Pistachio - 1 skein

Crochet Hook

☐ Size J-10 (6.00 mm)
or size needed for gauge

SIZE INFORMATION

Size: 36 x 52" (91.5 x 132 cm)

GAUGE INFORMATION

One pattern repeat (measured from 3-sc peak across to next 3-sc peak) to 2.5" [6.5 cm] measured over pattern using suggested hook or any size hook which will give the correct stitch gauge.

— STITCH GUIDE —

To change color, work last stitch of old color to last yarn over. Yarn over with new color and draw through all loops on hook to complete stitch. Proceed with new color. Fasten off old color. Take care to hide strands under side edging securely.

INSTRUCTIONS

Stripe Sequence:

Work colors for stripes in the following order:

Work *6 rows with Color A,
2 rows with Color B,
4 rows with Color A,
2 rows with Color C,
1 row with Color A,
2 rows with Color C,
4 rows with Color D,
3 rows with Color B,
2 rows with Color A,
2 rows with Color B,
2 rows with Color A,
3 rows with Color E,
1 row with Color F,
2 rows with Color E,
3 rows with Color F;
rep from * 3 times more,
then work 6 rows with Color A.

To Make: With Color A, ch 167.

Row 1: Work 2 sc in 2nd ch from hook, sc in each of next 4 ch, skip next 2 ch, sc in each of next 4 ch, *3 sc in next ch, sc in each of next 4 ch, skip next 2 ch, sc in each of next 4 ch; rep from * to last ch, 2 sc in last ch, turn - 15 ripples or patterns.

Row 2: Ch 1, 2 sc in first sc, sc in each of next 4 sc, skip next 2 sc, sc in each of next 4 sc, *3 sc in next sc, sc in each of next 4 sc, skip next 2 sc, sc in each of next 4 sc; rep from * to last sc, 2 sc in last sc turn.

Rows 3-6: Repeat Row 2, changing to Color B in last st of Row 6.

Rows 7 and 8: With Color B, rep Row 2 twice, changing to Color A in last st of Row 8.

Rows 9-162: Repeat Row 2 for pattern, changing colors as in Stripe Sequence, until all 162 rows of Stripe Sequence have been completed.

Do Not turn and Do Not fasten off after last row.

Side Edging: Using Color A, continue as follows:

Row 1: Ch 1, working in ends of rows, work sc evenly spaced along one side edge, turn.

Rows 2 and 3: Ch 1, sc in each sc across, turn.

Fasten off.

Rejoin Color A with sl st in opposite corner to work along rem side edge. Repeat Rows 1-3. Fasten off.

Weave in all ends.

Home For The Weekend Throw

■■■▢ INTERMEDIATE

SIZE INFORMATION

Size: 47 x 58" (119.5 x 147.5 cm)

GAUGE INFORMATION

One pattern repeat (measured
from peak to peak on ripple)
measures 7.5" [19 cm] across
and 10 rows to 6" [15 cm], using
suggested hook or any size hook
which will give the correct stitch
gauge.

STITCH GUIDE

dc5tog: [yo, insert hook in next
st, yo and draw up a loop, yarn
over and draw through 2 loops
on hook] 5 times, yo and draw
through all 6 loops on hook.

sc3tog: [insert hook into next st
and pull up a loop] 3 times, yarn
over and draw through all loops
on hook.

INSTRUCTIONS

Using MC, ch 160.

Row 1: (right side) Work 2 dc in
4th ch from hook (beg 3 ch count
as first dc), ch 2, skip next 2 ch,
dc in each of next 8 ch, dc5tog,
dc in each of next 8 ch, ch 2, *skip
next 2 ch, 5 dc in next ch, ch 2,
skip next 2 ch, dc in each of next 8
ch, dc5tog,
dc in each of next 8 ch, ch 2; rep
from * to last 3 ch, skip next 2 ch, 3
dc in last ch, changing to Color 1 in
last st, turn - 133 dc. Break MC.

Row 2: Using Color 1, ch 1, sc in
each of first 3 dc,
2 sc in next ch-2 sp, *sc in each dc
to next ch-2 sp, 2 sc in next ch-2
sp; rep from * across to last 3 dc,
sc in each of last 3 dc, changing to
MC in last st, turn - 157 sc. Break
Color 1.

Row 3: Using MC, ch 3 (counts as
dc throughout), 2 dc in same st, dc
in each of next 2 sts, ch 2,
skip next 2 sts, dc in each of next 6
sts, dc5tog,
dc in each of next 6 sts, ch 2,
*skip next 2 sts, dc in each of next
2 sts, 5 dc in next st,
dc in each of next 2 sts, ch 2,
skip next 2 sts, dc in each of next 6
sts, dc5tog,
dc in each of next 6 sts, ch 2; rep
from * to last 5 sts, skip next 2 sts,
dc in each of next 2 sts, 3 dc in last
st, changing to Color 1 in last st,
turn - 133 dc.
Break MC.

Row 4: Using Color 1, ch 1, sc in each of first 5 sts,

2 sc in next ch-2 sp, *sc in each dc to next ch-2 sp, 2 sc in next ch-2 sp; rep from * to last 5 sts,

sc in each of last 5 sts, changing to MC in last st, turn - 157 sc. Break Color 1.

Row 5: Using MC, ch 3, 2 dc in same st,

dc in each of next 4 sts, ch 2, skip next 2 sts,

dc in each of next 4 sts, dc5tog,

dc in each of next 4 sts, ch 2,

*skip next 2 sts, dc in each of next 4 sts, 5 dc in next st,

dc in each of next 4 sts, ch 2, skip next 2 sts,

dc in each of next 4 sts, dc5tog,

dc in each of next 4 sts, ch 2; rep from * to last 7 sts, skip next 2 sts, dc in each of next 4 sts, 3 dc in last st, changing to Color 1 in last st, turn - 133 dc. Break MC.

Row 6: Using Color 1, ch 1, sc in each dc and 2 sc in each ch-2 sp across, changing to MC in last st, turn - 157 sc. Break Color 1.

Row 7: Using MC, ch 3, 2 dc in same st,

dc in each of next 6 sts, ch 2, skip next 2 sts,

dc in each of next 2 sts, dc5tog,

dc in each of next 2 sts, ch 2,

*skip next 2 sts,

dc in each of next 6 sts,

5 dc in next st,

dc in each of next 6 sts, ch 2, skip next 2 sts,

dc in each of next 2 sts, dc5tog,

dc in each of next 2 sts, ch 2; rep from * to last 9 sts, skip next 2 sts,

dc in each of next 6 sts, 3 dc in last st, changing to Color 1 in last st, turn - 133 dc. Break MC.

Row 8: Using Color 1, rep Row 6.

Row 9: Using MC, ch 3, 2 dc in same st,

dc in each of next 8 sts, ch 2, skip next 2 sts, dc5tog, ch 2,

*skip next 2 sts,

dc in each of next 8 sts, 5 dc in next st, dc in each of next 8 sts, ch 2, skip next 2 sts, dc5tog, ch 2; rep from * to last 11 sts, skip next 2 sts, dc in each of next 8 sts, 3 dc in

last st, changing to Color 1 in last st, turn - 133 dc. Break MC.

Row 10: Using Color 1, rep Row 6.

Row 11: Using MC, ch 3, 2 dc in same st, ch 2, skip next 2 sts, dc in each of next 8 sts, dc5tog,

dc in each of next 8 sts, ch 2,

*skip next 2 sts,

5 dc in next st, ch 2, skip next 2 sts,

dc in each of next 8 sts, dc5tog,

dc in each of next 8 sts, ch 2; rep from * to last 3 sts, skip next 2 sts,

3 dc in last st, turn - 133 dc.

Rows 12-21: Using **MC only,** rep Rows 2-11, changing to Color 2 in last st worked on Row 21. Break MC.

Rows 22-31: Repeat Rows 2-11, using Color 2 in place of Color 1.

Rows 32-41: Using **MC only,** rep Rows 12-21, changing to Color 3 in last st of last row. Break MC.

Rows 42-51: Repeat Rows 2-11, using Color 3 in place of Color 1.

Rows 52-61: Using **MC only,** rep rows 12-21, changing to Color 2 in last st of last row worked. Break MC.

Rows 62-71: Repeat Rows 2-11, using Color 2 in place of Color 1.

Rows 72-81: Using **MC only,** rep Rows 2-11, changing to Color 1 in last st of last row worked. Break MC.

Rows 82-91: Repeat Rows 2-11, but do not change color and Do Not turn.

Border:

Note: It is easy to overlook one st at corners or after chain spaces, or add one st. The exact number of stitches in the border is not as important as being sure that when working increases (3 or 5 sc in one st or 5 dc in one st) and decreases (sc3tog or dc5tog), these line up correctly over previous rnds.

Rnd 1: Using MC, ch 3 (forms corner sp), now working down side edge, sc around ends of rows (space singles so they lay flat along the side, not puckering or rippling) to next corner, ch 3 (corner sp), working in unused loops of beg ch, sc in each st to next corner, ch 3 (corner sp), now working along other side, work sc as before to corner, ch 3 (last corner sp), sc in each st and 2 sc in each ch-2 sp across top edge to beg corner sp, join with sl st in base of beg ch-3. Break MC and fasten off.

Rnd 2: Join Color 1 with sl st in same corner sp, ch 1, 5 sc in same sp, *working in back loops only around, sc in each sc to next corner sp, 5 sc in corner sp, sc in each of next 11 sc, **ch 2, skip 2 sc, 5 sc through both loops of next sc only (over center of 5 dc group 2 rows below), ch 2, skip next 2 sc, sc in each of next 9 sc***, sc3tog, sc in each of next 9 sc; rep from ** to next corner sp, ending last rep at ***, sc in each of last 2 sc, 5 sc in corner sp, sc in each sc along side edge to next corner sp, 5 sc in corner sp, sc in each of next 12 sc, ****sc3tog, sc in each of next 9 sc#, ch 2, skip next 2 sc, 5 sc in both loops of next sc only (over center of 5-dc group 2 rows below), ch 2, skip next 2 sc, sc in each of next 9 sc; rep from **** across, ending last rep at #, sc in each of last 3 sc, join with sl st in first sc. Break Color 1 and fasten off.

Rnd 3: Join Color 2 with a sl st in 3rd sc of corner 5-sc group, ch 1, sc in same st, ch 3, skip next 2 sc, **working in back loops only,** sc in each sc to next corner, *ch 3, skip 2 sc, sc in next sc (3rd sc of corner), ch 3, skip 2 sc - corner made,* sc in each of next 10 sc, **2 sc in next ch-2 sp, sc in each of next 2 sc, 3 sc through both loops of next sc only, sc in each of next 2 sc, 2 sc in next ch-2 sp, sc in each of next 8 sc***, sc3tog, sc in each of next 8 sc; rep from ** across to next corner, ending last rep at ***, sc in each of last 3 sc, make corner,

sc in each sc across to next corner,

make corner,

sc in each of next 11 sc,

****sc3tog, sc in each of next 8

sc#,

2 sc in next ch-2 sp,

sc in each of next 2 sc,

3 sc through both loops of next sc

only, sc in each of next 2 sc,

2 sc in next ch-2 sp,

sc in each of next 8 sc;

rep from **** across, but ending

last rep at #,

sc in each of last 3 sc before

corner, ch 3,

join with sl st in first sc.

Break Color 2 and fasten off.

Rnd 4: Join Color 3 with sl st in last

ch-3 sp made,

(ch 3, 2 dc) in same sp, ch 2,

3 dc in next ch-3 sp, working in

back loops only,

dc in each sc to next corner, *3 dc in*

next ch-3 sp, ch 2, 3 dc in next ch-3

sp - **corner made,**

dc in each of next 10 sc,

**ch 2, skip next 2 sc,

dc in each of next 2 sc,

skip next sc,

5 dc through both loops of next sc

only, skip next sc,

dc in each of next 2 sc, ch 2,

skip next 2 sc,

dc in each of next 6 sc***,

dc5tog, dc in each of next 6 sc;

rep from ** across to next corner,

ending last rep at ***,

dc in each of last 4 sc, make corner,

dc in each sc to next corner,

make corner,

dc in each of next 9 sc,

****dc5tog,

dc in each of next 6 sc#, ch 2,

skip next 2 sc,

dc in each of next 2 sc,

skip next sc,

5 dc through both loops of next sc

only, skip next sc,

dc in each of next 2 sc, ch 2,

skip next 2 sc,

dc in each of next 6 sc; rep from

**** to next corner, ending last rep

at #, dc in each of last 2 sc,

join with sl st in first dc.

Break Color 3 and fasten off.

Rnd 5: Join MC with sl st in 1st

dc of corner, ch 1, sc in same st,

working in back loops only,

sc in each dc around, working 3 sc

in each corner ch-2 sp and 2 sc in

each rem ch-2 sp, join with sl st in

first sc. Break yarn and fasten off.

Weave in all ends neatly.

Lace Delight Throw

SHOPPING LIST

Yarn (Worsted Weight)

[6 ounces, 315 yards
(170 grams, 288 meters) per skein]:

☐ Color 1 Cottonwood - 3 skeins

☐ Color 2 Sea Mist - 2 skeins

   Desert Rose - 2 skeins

☐ Color 3 Deep Pine - 2 skeins

   Wild Raspberry - 2 skeins

Crochet Hook

☐ Size 7 (4.50 mm)
   or size needed for gauge

SIZE INFORMATION

Size: 45 x 50" (114.5 x 127 cm)

GAUGE INFORMATION

One repeat of 18 sts to 3.75" [9.5 cm] and one color stripe to 2" [5 cm], measured over pattern, using suggested hook or any size hook which will give the correct stitch gauge.

INSTRUCTIONS

Using Color 2, ch 218.

Row 1: Sc in 2nd ch from hook, ch 3, skip next 2 ch, sc in next ch, [ch 5, skip next 3 ch, sc in next ch] 3 times,

*[ch 3, skip next 2 ch, sc in next ch] twice, [ch 5, skip next 3 ch, sc in next ch] 3 times; rep from * across to last 3 ch, ch 3, skip next 2 ch, sc in last ch.

**Row 2: (right side) Ch 3 (counts as first dc), turn, dc in same st, ch 3, skip next ch-3 sp, sc in next ch-5 sp, 9 dc in next ch-5 sp, sc in next ch-5 sp, ch 3,

*skip next ch-3 sp, 3 dc in next st, ch 3, skip next ch-3 sp, sc in next ch-5 sp, 9 dc in next ch-5 sp, sc in next ch-5 sp, ch 3; rep from * across to last ch-3 sp, skip last ch-3 sp, 2 dc in last st.

Row 3: Ch 1, turn, sc in each of first 2 dc, ch 1, skip next ch-3 sp and next sc, [dc in next dc, ch 1] 9 times,

*skip next ch-3 sp, sc in each of next 3 dc, ch 1, skip next ch-3 sp and next sc, [dc in next dc, ch 1] 9 times; rep from * across to last ch-3 sp, skip last ch-3 sp, sc in each of last 2 dc.

Row 4: Ch 1, turn, sc in first sc, *skip next ch-1 sp, [dc in next ch, ch 1] 4 times, [dc, ch 1] twice in next dc, dc in next dc, [ch 1, dc in next dc] 3 times, skip next sc, sc in next sc; rep from * across, changing to Color 1 in last st.

Row 5: Using new color, ch 6 (counts as first dc and ch 3), skip next 2 dc, sc in next dc, [ch 5, skip next ch-1 sp, sc in next ch-1 sp] twice, ch 5, skip next ch-1 sp, sc in next dc, ch 3, skip next 2 dc, dc in next sc, *ch 3, skip next 2 dc, sc in next dc, [ch 5, skip next ch-1 sp, sc in next

ch-1 sp] twice,

ch 5, skip next ch-1 sp,

sc in next dc, ch 3,

skip next 2 dc, dc in next sc;

rep from * across.

Repeat Rows 2-5 for pattern,

working in the following color

sequence:

Using Color 1, work Rows 2-4,

changing to Color 3.

Using Color 3, work Rows 2-4,

changing to Color 1.

Using Color 1, work Rows 2-4,

changing to Color 2.**

Now rep from ** to ** 5 times

more.

Using Color 2, work Rows 2-4 once

more, Do Not change colors at the

end of Row 4.

Break yarn and fasten off.

Weave in all ends neatly.

Rippled Afghan

SHOPPING LIST

Yarn (DK/Sportweight)

[1.75 ounces, 160 yards
(50 grams, 146 meters) per ball]:

☐ Color 1   Dk Blue - 10 balls
☐ Color 2   Blue - 10 balls
☐ Color 3   Lt Blue - 10 balls

Crochet Hook

☐ Size I-9 (5.50 mm)
  or size needed for gauge

SIZE INFORMATION

Size: 50 x 72" (127 x 183 cm)

GAUGE INFORMATION

One repeat should measure 4.5"
[11.5 cm] measured over pattern,
using suggested hook or any size
hook, which will give the correct
stitch gauge.

INSTRUCTIONS

Using Color 1, ch 258.

Row 1: Sc in 2nd ch from hook, sc in next ch, skip next ch, [sc in each of next 10 ch, 3 sc in next ch, sc in each of next 10 ch, skip 2 ch] 10 times, sc in each of next 10 ch, 3 sc in next ch, sc in each of next 10 ch, skip one ch, sc in each of last 2 ch.

Row 2: Ch 1, turn, sc in each of next 2 sc **through both loops**, skip next sc, [sc in each of next 10 sc **through back loops only**, 3 sc in next sc, sc in each of next 10 sc **through back loops only**, skip next 2 sc] 10 times, sc in each of next 10 sc **through back loops only**, 3 sc in next sc, sc in each of next 10 sc **through back loops only**, skip next sc, sc in each of last 2 sc **through both loops**.

Repeat Row 2 six times more - 8 rows in all.

Change to Color 2 and rep Row 2 eight times.

Change to Color 3 and rep Row 2 eight times.

Now continue working in pattern and color sequence as set until piece measures approximately 72" [183 cm] from beg, ending after a Color 1 repeat.

Break yarn and fasten off.

Weave in all ends.

General Instructions

ABBREVIATIONS

"	inches
approx.	approximately
beg	begin or beginning
CC	Contrast Color
ch	chain
cm	centimeters
dc	double crochet
dec	decrease or decreasing
gm	gram
hdc	half double crochet
inc	increase or increasing
k	knit
MC	Main Color
mm	millimeter
rem	remain or remaining
rep	repeat
rnd(s)	round(s)
sc	single crochet
sl	slip
sp(s)	spaces(s)
st(s)	stitch(es)
tog	together
tr	treble crochet
yds	yards
yo	yarn over hook

* or # work instructions following or between * or # as many more times as indicated in addition to the first time.

() or [ ] work enclosed instructions as many times as specified by the number immediately following or work all enclosed instructions in the stitch or space indicated or contains explanatory remarks

___ the number(s) given after a hyphen at the end of a row or round denote(s) the number of stitches or spaces you should have on that row or round.

⬛◻◻◻ **BEGINNER**	Projects for first-time crocheters using basic stitches. Minimal shaping.
⬛⬛◻◻ **EASY**	Projects using yarn with basic stitches, repetitive stitch patterns, simple color changes, and simple shaping and finishing.
⬛⬛⬛◻ **INTERMEDIATE**	Projects using a variety of techniques, such as basic lace patterns or color patterns, mid-level shaping and finishing.
⬛⬛⬛⬛ **EXPERIENCED**	Projects with intricate stitch patterns, techniques and dimension, such as non-repeating patterns, multi-color techniques, fine threads, small hooks, detailed shaping and refined finishing.

Yarn Weight Symbol & Names	1 SUPER FINE	2 FINE	3 LIGHT	4 MEDIUM	5 BULKY	6 SUPER BULKY
Type of Yarns in Category	Sock, Fingering Baby	Sport, Baby	DK, Light Worsted	Worsted, Afghan Aran	Chunky, Craft, Rug	Bulky, Roving
Crochet Gauge* Ranges in Single Crochet to 4" (10 cm)	21-32 sts	16-20 sts	12-17 sts	11-14 sts	8-11 sts	5-9 sts
Advised Hook Size Range	B-1 to E-4	E-4 to 7	7 to I-9	I-9 to K-10.5	K-10.5 to M-13	M-13 and larger

*GUIDELINES ONLY: The chart above reflects the most commonly used gauges and hook sizes for specific yarn categories.

CROCHET HOOKS												
Metric mm	2.25	2.75	3.25	3.5	3.75	4	5	5.5	6	6.5	9	10	15
U.S.	B-1	C-2	D-3	E-4	F-5	G-6	H-8	I-9	J-10	K-10.5	N	P	Q

CROCHET TERMINOLOGY		
UNITED STATES		INTERNATIONAL
slip stitch (slip st)	=	single crochet (sc)
single crochet (sc)	=	double crochet (dc)
half double crochet (hdc)	=	half treble crochet (htr)
double crochet (dc)	=	treble crochet (tr)
treble crochet (tr)	=	double treble crochet (dtr)
double treble crochet (dtr)	=	triple treble crochet (ttr)
triple treble crochet (ttr)	=	quadruple treble crochet (qtr)
skip	=	miss

Slip Knot

1. Make a loop, then hook another loop through it.

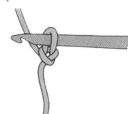

2. Tighten gently and slide the knot up to the hook.

Chain Stitch (ch)

1. Yarn over hook (yo) and draw the yarn through to form a new loop without tightening up the previous one.

2. Repeat to form as many chains (ch) as required. Do not count the slip knot as a stitch.

Slip Stitch (sl st)

This is the shortest crochet stitch and unlike other stitches is not used on its own to produce a fabric. It is used for joining, shaping and where necessary carrying the yarn to another part of the fabric for the next stage.

Insert hook into work (second chain from hook), yarn over hook (yo) and draw the yarn through both the work and loop on hook in one movement.

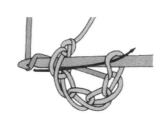

To join a chain ring with a slip stitch (sl st), insert hook into first chain (ch), yarn over hook (yo) and draw through both the work and the yarn on hook in one movement.

Single Crochet (sc)

1. Insert the hook into the work (2nd chain (ch) from hook on starting chain), yarn over hook (yo) and draw yarn through the work only.

2. Yarn over hook (yo) again and draw the yarn through both loops on the hook.

3. 1 single crochet (sc) made. Insert hook into next stitch: repeat (rep) from * in step 1.

Half Double Crochet (hdc)

1. Yarn over hook (yo) and insert the hook into the work (3rd chain (ch) from hook on starting chain) and draw through the work only.

2. Yarn over hook (yo) again and draw through all three loops on the hook.

3. 1 hdc made. Yarn over hook (yo), insert hook into next stitch (st), repeat (rep) from step 2.

Double Crochet (dc)

1. Yarn over hook (yo) and insert the hook into the work (4th chain from hook on starting chain).

2. Yarn over hook (yo) and draw through the work only.

3. Yarn over hook (yo) and draw through the first two loops only.

4. Yarn over hook (yo) and draw through the last two loops on the hook.

5. 1 dc made. Yarn over hook (yo), insert hook into next stitch (st); repeat (rep) from step 2.

Yarn Information

Projects in this book were made with medium or sportweight yarns. Any brand of yarn may be used. It is best to refer to yardage/meters when determining how many balls or skeins to purchase. Remember, to arrive at the finished size, it is the GAUGE/TENSION that is important, not the brand of yarn. For your convenience, listed below are the specific yarn ranges used to create our photographed models.

To The Point Throw
Mary Maxim's® Best Value

Optic Waves Throw
Mary Maxim's® Best Value

Autum Waves Throw
Mary Maxim's® Best Value

Rippled Lace Throw
Mary Maxim's® Best Value

Bands of Lace Ripple
Mary Maxim's® Best Value

Ocean Breeze Afghan
Mary Maxim's® Starlette

Rise and Fall Throw
Caron® Simply Soft®

Home For The Weekend Throw
Mary Maxim's® Starlette Ragg
Mary Maxim's® Starlette

Lace Delight Throw
Mary Maxim's® Best Value

Rippled Afghan
Mary Maxim's® Ultra Mellowspun